STORIES FROM HISTORY SERIES

EDITED BY JOHN LANG

STORIES FROM
THE CRUSADES

Wherever the battle was hottest, Richard seems to spring from the ground.

STORIES FROM
THE CRUSADES

BY

JANET HARVEY KELMAN

WITH PICTURES BY

L. D. LUARD

YESTERDAY'S CLASSICS
CHAPEL HILL, NORTH CAROLINA

Cover and arrangement © 2005 Yesterday's Classics.

This edition, first published in 2005 by Yesterday's Classics, is an unabridged republication of the work originally published by T. C. & E. C. Jack in 1907. The color illustrations by L. D. Luard in that volume are rendered in black and white in this edition. For a listing of the books published by Yesterday's Classics, please visit www.yesterdaysclassics.com. Yesterday's Classics is the publishing arm of the Baldwin Project which presents the complete text of dozens of classic books for children at www.mainlesson.com under the editorship of Lisa M. Ripperton and T. A. Roth.

ISBN-10: 1-59915-054-9

ISBN-13: 978-1-59915-054-3

Yesterday's Classics
PO Box 3418
Chapel Hill, NC 27515

TO

KATHARINE AND BARBARA

THE HEROES OF THE CRUSADES

The stories in this book are of heroes who lived hundred of years ago. They caught sight of a beautiful dream and lived and died to make it come true.

Their eagerness swept along with them not only men who had never dreamed the dream and who did not know for what end they fought, but bad men also who only wished to get what they could for themselves.

The Crusades are long past, yet to-day there are men who see visions of good and who wish to bring them down to earth. With them are others who fight selfishly as did Bohemond and Baldwin long ago. But there are still men like Francis, who carry goodwill with them, and great knights like Tancred and like Louis, who live to fight for the poor and the weak.

CONTENTS

I. How Peter Preached of Jerusalem   1

II. How Tancred Fought under the Banner of the Cross   12

III. How the Kings Fought for Glory and Not for Christ   36

IV. How Frederick Came to His Kingdom   56

V. How Louis Thought Death a Little Thing   63

CHAPTER I
HOW PETER PREACHED OF JERUSALEM

Once upon a time there was an ugly little boy called Peter, who lived in his father's castle in France. He was a restless boy, and liked always to do or to hear something new. His home was very quiet, for his father was a great fighter, and was often away at the wars for months at a time.

But though one day was very like another in Peter's life when he was young, he used to hear tales of pilgrimage and of battle that made him long to be free to go out into the world himself.

The country round his home and in the other northern lands near it was bare and and the towers and walls of the cities were gloomy, but the boy heard of other lands and other cities. He heard that in Byzantium, where the Greek Emperor had his palace, the houses were built of marble, and their walls were lined with gold, and that in the lands around it rich fruits and grain grew. He often heard of another city called Jerusalem, for many pilgrims went to it because it was at Jerusalem that Jesus Christ died. Hundreds of years before Peter was born, Helena, the mother of the Greek Emperor Constantine, found a cross which she thought must be the Cross on which Christ died. She was full of awe and wonder, and in order that all who served Christ might see the Cross, it was set up in Jerusalem on the spot where it was thought to have stood when Christ died upon it. Long after Constantine and his mother were dead, a king who did not serve Christ carried the Cross away from Jerusalem. The Emperor who then reigned in Greece fought with this king for ten years before he could subdue him. At last he won the cross again, and with it lands and gold, but these gave him far less joy than the thought that the cross would again stand in Jerusalem. He kept part of it in his city of Byzantium; with the rest he went to Jerusalem. He was a great man and a proud man, but he was humble when he thought of the cross and of what it told of the death of Christ. So he took off his beautiful clothes, and with bare feet and wearing a plain robe he carried the cross up the street of Jerusalem, and set it once more within the church that had been built where Christ died.

When Peter was young, hundreds of pilgrims went to Jerusalem to worship at the foot of this cross. They did so for many reasons. Some did it because they loved the thought of Christ and wished to stand where He had stood, and to see the land in which He had lived. Others went because they thought it would make other people think them very good. They hoped to be great people when they came back to their homes again. But the largest number went because the Pope and the priests told them that those who went in poverty to the

Holy City would be forgiven for all the wrong things they had done. Many a man who was very unhappy because he had killed some one by stealth, gave up all that he had and went with nothing except a staff to visit the cross.

These pilgrims were often very cruelly treated in Jerusalem, for men called Saracens who did not serve Christ lived and ruled there, and they made each pilgrim give them money before they would allow him into the city. They are sometimes called "Moslems," and they were followers of a prophet named Mahomet. They were cruel to the Christians who lived in Jerusalem, as well as to the pilgrims who came to it.

Once, when Hakem, who was called "the mad Sultan," ruled in Jerusalem, the streets of the city surged with an angry throng. The white robes of the soldiers of Hakem flashed out amongst the bright colours that were worn by men of other Moslem races. Every face was full of scorn and anger. Harsh voices cursed those who served Christ. Jews hid in corners and alleys that they might not suffer with the Christians, for them too the Moslems hated.

The Moslems call their churches mosques, and the reason of their great anger on this day was that they had found a dead dog lying in a mosque. They thought that this had done such harm to their mosque that they could not pray in it till they had made it pure again, and they were sure that a Christian had thrown the dog's body there in order to annoy them. The news spread through the town, and each moment the crowd grew larger and more fierce.

"Let us fall on the Christian dogs!" they shouted. "Let us kill them without mercy!" "Who are they that they should soil our temple?"

The Christians had gathered into one place in sorrow and in fear. They all wore clothes of dull dingy shades, because they were not allowed to wear beautiful colours nor white robes like Hakem's soldiers. Each of them wore a leather thong to show that the Moslems ruled over him. Their hearts were more gloomy than their robes. If they were all killed, the Christian Church would have no one left in Jerusalem. They waited in terror. But the noise they heard was not what they had feared. A clear voice rang out. The man who spoke was one of themselves. His name was Olindo.

"Nothing could be a greater evil," he said, "than that the Church should perish. I will die for you and for our faith. Do not forget me nor my people."

The others burst into tears, but though they were sad to think of Olindo's death, no one tried to stay him. He passed swiftly out from them, and met the Moslem leaders as they hurried on to kill the Christians.

"I alone am guilty of this deed," said Olindo; and he had not time to say more, for he fell dead in the street, killed by the swords of those nearest to him.

At that time those who were called Christians were quarrelling with each other. There were two Churches. One was the Greek Church, the other was the Church of Rome. The Popes, who reigned in Rome, always wished to make the Greek Church obey them, so that there might be only one Christian Church. And when Peter lived it seemed that perhaps this dream of

HOW PETER PREACHED

the Popes might come true. A fierce race of men called Turks had swept westward from the Great Wall of China. Everything had fallen before them except the faith of the Prophet whom the Moslems followed. It did not fall, because, instead of trying to fight it, the Turks took it for their own. It suited them well, because it taught that whoever died fighting for it, against those who did not obey Mahomet, would go straight to heaven. So instead of making slaves of the Moslems whom they had defeated, the Turks joined their armies to their own and led them against the Empire of Greece. That was why the Pope who lived then thought he might be able to unite Rome and Greece once more. Greece asked Rome to help her against the Turks, and Rome hoped that if she helped her so, then Greece would be willing to do what she wished afterwards.

And it was of these things that men who knew the world talked and thought when Peter was a boy. As he grew up, he longed to have a share in all the great things that were being done in the world, and in order to know about them he entered the home of the Bishop of Paris that he might be a priest, and so have time to read many books. But he soon found that he could not be happy while he only read about what other men had done. He yearned to do things himself. The bishop liked him well and wished to keep him with him, but the restless lad would not stay. He went to fight in Flanders, but it was only for a short time that war seemed gay and pleasant to him. He was made a prisoner, and he found a cell far more dull and dreary than his study in Paris.

Then he escaped from prison, and made a home of his own. There he and his wife Beatrice lived for a few years together, but soon she died and left Peter with three little children. Peter gave the care of the children to a friend and fled to a hermit's cell. It seemed to him that he had tried every kind of life in vain, and that nothing was left him but to live alone and to think and pray till death came to him.

But Peter was neither old nor ill, and death was a long way off from him. The narrow cell became a prison to him, and he grew restless as a lion in a cage. But he had vowed that he would live the life of a hermit, and if death would not come to him to bring him freedom, there was only one way in which he could keep his vow and yet do things and take part in the life of the world. That way was to go on pilgrimage. As he thought of this, the old light flashed in his keen dark eyes.

"I too," he said to himself, "will walk barefoot where Christ has trod. My tears shall fall on His grave, and I will kneel before the cross."

He set out on his journey, and after many risks and dangers he reached Jerusalem. Peter had seen many beautiful towns and rich valleys, and when he saw the bare rocky ground that led up to Jerusalem, he was amazed that Christ had died in so dreary a city.

"How strange," thought he, "that the Lord of All should have chosen this barren spot!" As he went from place to place in the city he was in great excitement. He made such vivid pictures in his mind of all that had happened there that the thought of it took away his breath, and he longed that he might die where such things had taken place. It was dreadful for him to see

HOW PETER PREACHED

how those who cared not for the memory of Christ scorned and defiled the holy places, and robbed and ill-treated the pilgrims who asked only to be allowed to worship and to think in peace. He sought out the head of the Christian Church, whom men called the Patriarch of Jerusalem, and talked with him of what might be done to save the Holy City from the Moslems, and he told the Christians in Jerusalem that he would go away and bring the people of Europe to fight for the Holy City.

On the evening before Peter left Jerusalem he went into the church in which the cross stood, to pray. He was weary with talk and thought and with many visits to holy places, and he fell asleep. While he slept, he thought he saw Christ come to him and say:

"Arise, Peter, do with courage that which thou hast said. I will be with thee."

Peter rose from his knees in great joy. He left Jerusalem and went with haste to Rome. There the Pope listened to him gladly and gave him his blessing. He told him to go from town to town and from land to land, and to tell every one who would listen, of the sufferings of pilgrims and of the dishonour that was shown to the memory of Christ in the places where He had once walked.

This was a different kind of life from the one Peter had lived in the hermit's cell. It was full of change and excitement, and it had in it the great hope that one day he would see Jerusalem in the hands of Christian armies, and pilgrims welcomed and honoured where they had suffered so much.

Peter was still ugly. He was small and ungainly, but he had piercing black eyes, and those who caught sight of them forgot to look at anything else. He was not fifty years old, but the hard life he had lived had turned his hair and beard white. He did not wear either hat or shoes. As he rode along on his mule, the long coarse folds of his robe flapped round his bare feet, and the cord that bound his waist dangled at his side. In his hands he carried a heavy crucifix.

When he stopped and began to speak, people thought he was some silly, worthless man, but before he had spoken many sentences they gathered close to him and listened with open eyes and mouths, for the ugly little man could make other men see the things he saw, and feel what he felt. Everywhere Peter made men and women think that the only thing that mattered in the whole world was to save Jerusalem from the Moslems.

The crowds of people who followed Peter soon grew as excited as he was himself. They thought that he was so holy, that if they touched him or pulled a hair from his mule's tail, they would be better and happier.

When Peter had told hundreds of people about Jerusalem, the Pope himself came to meet as many of them as could be gathered together to hear him. The city to which he asked them to come could not hold the crowds who came together from every side. It was winter, and bitterly cold, and knights and nobles, monks and workmen, camped in the icy fields round the town.

When the great day came, the Pope sat on a throne in the city square with Peter by his side. Peter told once more of Jerusalem and of what he had seen there; and when he was silent the Pope rose and promised that however wicked were any of those who heard him, yet if they would only now go to fight in the Holy War he would promise that no evil would ever come to them because of the wrong things they had done in the past, and that when they died they would go straight to heaven.

The people had been greatly excited by Peter's speech, and as they heard the Pope promise such wonderful things to all who would fight for Jerusalem, they began to shout out, "It is the will of God: it is the will of God."

"It is the will of God," answered the Pope. "Let that be your battle-cry. And because ye seek to save the city of our Lord, let the cross be your sign. Wear it on your shoulders and on your breasts. With it, ye shall certainly be either victors or martyrs."

Then nobles with their gay banners and flashing armour, and peasants in coarse dull-coloured tunics, crowded forward to take the red cross of war from the hands of the Pope.

After this, many others besides Peter went out to preach the Crusade, and all along the roads by which they went, there gathered groups of men, women, and children, each with the sign of the cross on shoulder or banner.

The knights and nobles who had taken the cross had many things to do ere they could leave their lands. They had to sell jewels and silver dishes that they might have money to pay for the food their followers would need on the journey and throughout the fighting. They

Peter set off with an unruly band of men.

had to find people in whose care they could leave children and castles. But many foolish folk who knew nothing at all of what it meant to go on foot to the Holy Land, or to fight the fierce Turkish soldiers, and who had nothing to leave behind, crowded round Peter and begged him to wait for no one, but to lead them at once to the Holy City. Peter knew nothing of war, and although he did know something of the danger of the journey, he did not think how much more hard it would

HOW PETER PREACHED

be to find food for a thousand people than for one. He thought, too, that all those men whose eager faces looked up into his, were as much in earnest as he was himself, and would be as willing to suffer and even to die. Besides all that, he was not at all patient himself. He wished to see the banner of the Cross floating from the walls of Jerusalem, and he wished to see it at once. He could hardly bear to think of the long march that must lie between him and victory, so it is no wonder that he would not wait for the armies of the nobles, but set off with a great unruly band of men who had not learned to fight nor even to obey!

Few of them ever reached the Holy Land. When Peter brought the handful that still followed him to Byzantium, where the Greek Emperor reigned, they behaved so badly that the Emperor was sorry that he had asked for help from Rome. He hated the thought of the armies of the Holy War, before any of the real warriors had come to his land.

CHAPTER II

HOW TANCRED FOUGHT UNDER THE BANNER OF THE CROSS

While Peter led these wild lawless men to Byzantium, the nobles who had vowed to fight in the Holy War were preparing to lead out the armies of the first Crusade. There were many brave knights ready to fight for Jerusalem. One of the bravest was Godfrey, who came from Germany. When he was at peace with those around him, he had all the charm of winning manners and of gentle voice, but in battle he was brave and dreadful, and as strong as a raging lion. Once he had fought for the Emperor of Germany against the Pope, and ever since that time he had been very unhappy, because the only thing he feared was the power of the Church. He was delighted when he heard of the preaching of Peter. To save Jerusalem seemed to him a splendid thing, and then he thought that no harm would come to him because he had fought against the Pope, if he should be able to win the Holy City for Rome and for the Christian faith. Two of his brothers joined him, and many other lords and nobles came to set out with him for Jerusalem.

But all his followers were not men who had lived in courts. There were many workmen and peasants, and some wild men in shaggy clothes who came from the Scottish shores, and who found their way to his camp by making the sign of the cross with their fingers. Every one knew what that meant, and pointed out the way to the strangers.

Another knight gathered an army in Italy. His name was Bohemond. He was as brave and as clever as Godfrey, but he was not like him in any other thing, except perhaps that both men were tall and handsome. Bohemond wished to win land for himself. Above all, he wanted the land and the wealth of the Greek Emperor. When he heard of the Crusade, he thought that it would be easy for him to find an excuse to seize the lands of Greece if he could quarrel with the Emperor about the Crusade. But he did not tell his soldiers that. Though he cared very little about Jerusalem or about the wood of the Cross, he could speak as stirringly about them as Peter had done, and one day when he had spoken of these things to his brother's army he tore his great red banner into strips, and made crosses for all the soldiers who would take them.

With Bohemond there rode his cousin Tancred, and amongst them all there was none so faithful to him as Tancred. This was wonderful, because Tancred was "a very perfect gentle knight," and many of the things Bohemond did must have been hateful to him.

When the Greek Emperor asked for help from Rome, he wished the Pope to send men to fight under his banner and to win battles for him. He could make no use of the rabble that had come to Byzantium with Peter. But when the real armies of the Crusade poured into the fields around the city he was filled with fear. These strong gay knights with the warriors who followed them were far worse than useless to him. He knew something of the bareness of the land that lay round their castles, and of the rugged life that even the noblest of them lived in their northern homes. And he was sure that the rich plains of his country, and his cities with their marble palaces would make many of the knights wish to win them from him, and that they would never be content to fight only for the freedom of the Holy Land.

It was no wonder that he was afraid. As the Crusaders gazed up at the walls of Byzantium, it seemed to them like an enchanted city. The fields and orchards around it were richly laden with corn and fruit. The buildings within it rose amongst bright and beautiful gardens, higher and higher towards the gilded roof of the palace, above which, three domes shone in the warm sunshine. Not far off stood the Church of St. Sophia, and in it too were gold and gems. Ships lay on the sparkling waters of the Golden Horn beyond the city, and the sun shone brightly on the narrow sea that lay between Europe and Asia.

When Bohemond and Tancred came to Byzantium, they found that some of the armies that had already arrived were on one side of the narrow sea and some were on the other. Tancred was very eager to see all the armies on the side away from Byzantium and towards Jerusalem, but he found that the Emperor would not lend them ships in which to cross the water, until all the leaders had promised that they would make him the ruler over every town that they won from the Moslems.

The knights were very angry. They had always kept for themselves the cities they had fought for and won, and they could not bear the thought of winning Jerusalem only to give it up again. But the Emperor was a crafty man. When he saw that he could make them promise what he wished by fair means, he made up his mind that other ways might succeed where these had failed. He took many of the Crusaders over the narrow sea, for he was afraid of having too many of them close to Byzantium. Then when he had divided them from each other, he tried to win his will.

He feasted the knights at his palace and made them believe that he thought them great and noble people. He really scorned them very much, because though they were brave, they did not care about learning or art. But he tried to hide from them the scorn that he and his people felt for them. He spoke to Godfrey about the grave where the body of Christ had lain, and about the wood of the true Cross, till Godfrey really thought he was a man who cared as much about Jerusalem as he himself did, and said that he would think of him as his Emperor. And that was what the crafty Greek wished, for he cared nothing at all for the Holy City. But he did not speak to Bohemond about Jerusalem! He led him through the palace, and as they walked they passed an open door. Bohemond looked in and started in surprise, for he saw that gems and gold and silver were piled in disorder, while here and there he saw the leg of a costly table or the back of an inlaid chair.

"Ah," said Bohemond, "what victories he might win who owns all this!"

"It is your own," a voice whispered to him.

Bohemond said he could not take so great a treasure, but though he said that, he was very glad indeed to get it, and at night, all that had dazzled his eyes as he glanced through the open door, lay in his own tent. He said, of course, that he would do what the Emperor wished, but though the Emperor was glad to have him say it, in order that other knights might be more willing to say so too, he knew very well that Bohemond would not keep his promise a day longer than he wished to do so.

The Emperor wished all the knights to own his rule, but there was one who would not. It was Tancred. He hated the silly round of pleasure in Byzantium. He scorned both the gold and the flattering words of the Emperor. One day a Greek nobleman spoke rudely to him, and Tancred struck him in the public street. After that his life was in danger. He took off his glittering armour, put on the dress of a common soldier, and escaped across the narrow sea to that part of the army that had already gone over. But still the Emperor would not let the others go without Tancred's promise. At last Bohemond went to Tancred and said to him that he was to blame, because he alone was keeping the army back and standing in the way of the rescue of the Holy City by refusing to serve the Emperor. Tancred still had faith in his cousin, and when he pled with him he could not

HOW TANCRED FOUGHT

say no. So he yielded; only he hoped that the Emperor would soon break his promise to help the Crusaders so that they might be free from their promise to him. Then the Emperor lent his ships and hastened the Crusaders on their way with gifts and promises, but he sent messengers to warn the Saracens that they were coming to attack them. The great army that marched into Asia knew nothing of that. There were a hundred thousand horsemen, besides many, many others. It is not possible to imagine the noise they made. The heavy armour of the horses rattled and clashed, and the clang of armour drowned the sound of trampling. Often a peal of merry laughter rang out from a group of village children, or from some gay lady who had come with father or husband to share the danger and the triumph of the Holy War. As they rode, the trumpets sounded and the deep voices of the heralds shouted, "Save the Holy Sepulchre!" The sunlight flashed from bright weapons and from gay scarfs and banners.

They marched gladly on till the city of Nicæa rose before them. Its walls were so broad and so strong that horses could dash round on the top without doing any harm. And three hundred towers guarded the city. On one side, the water of a lake washed close up to the wall: on the other, mountains rose from it. The black flag of the Turk waved every here and there on the steep slope, and the tents of Moslem soldiers clustered round each flag.

For seven weeks the Crusaders laid siege to the city. During those days there was a great deal of fighting with the Turks outside the wall. Tancred was always in the thick of the battle, and ever where he was, the army of the Holy Cross carried all before it, and the enemy fled to their tents. But the city still held out, and from its walls arrows and stones hurtled down with deadly aim. There was one huge Moslem who never seemed to miss his mark. He hurled stones and arrows and javelins, and wherever they fell they brought death. One day he grew so bold that he threw away his shield and stood on the wall and scorned his foes beneath. A hundred bows were stretched tight, a hundred arrows whizzed through the air, but when they had all fallen to earth, he still stood there unharmed. It seemed as if he bore a charmed life. But he had insulted the armies of the Cross, and Godfrey had heard him do it. A thrill went through the camp as the German leader raised his bow and arrow. No other arm was raised. Godfrey's arrow sped alone through the air. A breathless moment passed. Then the body of the giant fell forward from the wall, dead, shot through the heart, into the moat below.

The knights could not understand how it was that the people in Nicæa were not suffering from hunger. Those who shot down the stones and the arrows looked strong and well. Yet the armies had watched the gates night and day for seven weeks. At last they found out that when night fell and there was no moon, food was brought to Nicæa across the lake and pulled up into the city. At first it seemed as if nothing could be done to stop this, but at last a plan was made. The lake stretched away from Nicæa till only a strip of land lay between it and the narrow sea. The Crusaders sent messengers to the Emperor and asked him to give them ships and sledges. This he gladly did, because he wished them to think that he meant to help them in all their battles. Then in the darkness when all was ready, a band of knights spurred their horses to the narrow sea. They hoisted the ships on to the sledges and dragged them over the sandy ridge, and then launched the vessels in the lake. When the daylight came and the Moslems looked out, they saw their enemies' ships riding under the walls of their city and knew that no help could come to them by land or sea.

The Crusaders were delighted. "Only a few more hours," they thought, "and Nicæa must be in our hands."

In a few more hours Nicæa had fallen, but the flag that floated from its towers was the flag of Greece. Every one was full of anger and surprise. The soldiers gathered round the knights.

"What does it mean?" they asked.

But the knights could not tell them. By some means two Greek generals had entered Nicæa and had made the people there believe that it would be much better for them to yield to the Emperor than to the armies from the North.

But though the Crusaders were very angry, they did not stay to grieve that Nicæa was not their own. They were glad, because they had subdued so strong a city. They hastened on and broke into two bands that they might more easily find food. But Turks on swift horses watched them and rode back to tell their chief how carelessly the Crusaders marched. The land was beautiful and rich, and Bohemond gave the command to halt by a river that flowed through a grassy plain amongst clumps of trees. Everything seemed quiet and peaceful. Tancred listened to the heralds as they shouted three times over, "Save the Holy Sepulchre!" and thought with joy that soon there might be no need for the heralds' shout. But another cry ran through the tents! "The enemy is on us!" Ere men had time to arm, the clouds of dust beyond the river and the white turbans and green vests that flashed through the dust, proved to every man that the cry was true.

Arrows fell thick as rain. They glanced from the chain-mail of the knights, but they entered the joints of the horses' armour and made them frantic with pain. The horns and drums and terrible yells of the Turks maddened the horses still more. The Arab horses were lighter and swifter than those of the knights. They could dart away when the Crusaders attacked them and rush in again to attack in return.

Tancred was nearly killed. He had seen his brother fall. It may have made him reckless. Bohemond's sharp eyes saw that he was in the midst of foemen and that his lance was broken. He dashed across the river, swooped down on the Turks with a terrific yell, and bore Tancred safely away.

But while the Crusaders were fighting, another band of Turks fell on the camp and took it. The knights could not retake the camp and keep the foe at bay at the same time. They had no thought of yielding, but they saw that many of their followers were losing courage. Suddenly they heard a shout of joy. Godfrey and his warriors were in sight. The voices of the priests led the battle cry, "It is the will of God! It is the will of God!"

HOW TANCRED FOUGHT

The Turks were tired with the long fight. They could not resist this new force. They were overcome, chased, and slain. Their camp fell into the Crusaders' hands. The knights found strange new weapons there, and many camels and horses. They handled the curious Eastern arms in wonder, and led the camels about in delight.

But a great danger was before them. A band of Turks had escaped. They had not been able to conquer their foes, but they could injure them still. They rode swiftly forward and burned the towns and trampled the corn in the fields along the roads by which the Crusaders would have to go. They rode forward for five hundred miles, and behind them they left empty houses and barren lands.

It was the hottest part of the year, and as the armies marched through this wasted land, men and horses dropped out of the ranks to die of thirst. So many horses died, that the stores had to be carried by dogs and by goats.

One day during this terrible time, some one noticed wet sand on the paws of a dog. Then another was found with wet sand on his coat. The excitement was terrible. Every one searched for the footprints of the dogs that they might find the water the dogs had found. At last the tracks were seen, and thousands of weak and thirst-stricken soldiers tottered up to the mountain stream in which the dogs had bathed. But they drank so wildly that three hundred of them died by the bank of the torrent.

As the Crusaders rode south towards Jerusalem, they overtook bands of Turks. Some of these Moslem warriors went into the towns for shelter, and the knights often followed them there and took away their weapons.

One day Tancred led his followers into the town of Tarsus and raised his flag to show that it belonged to him, but just after he had done this, Baldwin, one of Godfrey's brothers, rode up to Tancred and said that he and his men must have half of the spoil of the city. But the people of Tarsus were Christians, and Tancred would not let his own knights take any of their wealth from them, so he could not allow Baldwin to rob them either. But Baldwin would not listen to him. He forced his way into the town, tore down Tancred's banner and flung it into a ditch.

Tancred was very angry, and so were his men. They loved him and boasted of his brave deeds, and they were enraged that any one should treat him so. They wished to fight Baldwin at once and chase him from Tarsus. But Tancred pled with them not to attack another Crusader. He spoke of the Holy War and of Jerusalem, and led them out from the town they had won and on to Malmistra. But Baldwin did not find as much as he wished in Tarsus, and before long, Tancred's soldiers saw the banners of the man they hated beneath the walls of Malmistra. This time Tancred yielded to his soldiers, and marched out against Baldwin, but he had no heart to fight against one with whom he had set out to save the Holy City, and next morning the two knights met in friendship before their men and vowed to forget the past.

HOW TANCRED FOUGHT

Tancred had no more trouble from the greed and meanness of Baldwin, for Godfrey's brother stole away in the dead of night with a band of picked fighting men, left the crusading army, and marched off to win an empire for himself.

At last, after months of weary marching, the Crusaders stood on a spur of the rocky hills over which the last part of their track had lain, and looked down on the rich valley of the Orontes River. They saw vineyards and cornfields on either side of the river, and shut in between it and the mountains, they saw the town of Antioch. It was a beautiful town and a very strong one, with a great citadel that rose high above its walls. It was called "The Queen of the East." Soon the Crusaders had made their camp in the fair green valley. The sun shone on white tents and flashing weapons, on bucklers of gold and green and crimson, and on the gay banners of the knights.

The men were weary with the long march and with the hunger and thirst they had so often suffered. Instead of closing round the city, they spread over the valley and feasted. They dreamed of all that they meant to do instead of doing anything.

It was autumn, and the weather was warm and sunny. The vines were heavy with clusters of grapes. Cattle fed in the pasture lands and corn grew in the fields. Sometimes bands of Moslems from the city fell on the Crusaders as they feasted. Then the knights mounted and fought, and won great glory for themselves, but the town was as safe as ever.

But when winter came and the camp was a marsh, they saw how foolish it was to kill all the cattle and feast on corn and wine, and waste it, when, if they had been careful, they might have had more than enough for the wet days of winter, and might even have been within Antioch.

Tancred and his men rode far and near to find food for the army, and then he stood by in wrath when he saw that the stores he had fought so hard to win were wasted, as the fruit of the valley had been. Many men grew hopeless, and tried to steal away from the army by night. Tancred was always ready either to fight or to help. One night as he watched by the camp, he saw two figures clambering up the hillside. He thought he knew one of them. He spurred his horse up the steep road and caught them. One was a knight and the other was Peter the Hermit! He had thought it would be so simple to win the Holy City, and now the long waiting and the carelessness of those around him had sapped all his courage, and Peter had fled. But when Tancred brought him back, he vowed on the Gospels that he would never leave the army again till Jerusalem was won.

At last the Crusaders did enter Antioch, but it was not by the strength of their arms. Tancred's cousin, Bohemond, made a plot with one of the tower-keepers of the city. But when he told the knights of it, he said that he would not lead them into Antioch unless they would give it to him to be his own. At first they would not agree to this. They did not like his stealthy plans, and they did not wish him to be Lord of Antioch. But

HOW TANCRED FOUGHT

soon they heard that a Moslem army was coming to fight with them and to help Antioch, so they yielded.

The night on which they chose to enter was wild and stormy. The knights and soldiers heard the wind rush down the valleys. They saw tents and walls and towers gleam out in the sudden lightning flashes and then sink into utter darkness again. The tower-keeper lowered a ladder, but every one shrank back from it.

Bohemond led the way himself.

The Crusaders were warriors, not robbers, and the storm made it seem as if uncanny powers of air were fighting against their unsoldierly deed. Bohemond, however, was not afraid to be mean. When he saw that no one else would go, he led the way himself. Sixty knights followed him. They opened the city gates, and soon the crusading army rushed through the streets of Antioch. But the citadel was so strong and so well defended that the armies of the knights could not take it.

The foolish soldiers feasted on the food they found in the city. They did not know that the Moslem armies were at their gates till they saw the horses dashing through the camp that they had left. In a few days the food was done. The enemy was in the citadel and in the valley. Many Crusaders tried to flee. The others called them rope-dancers because they slipped from the city wall on ropes. They were less afraid of the Turkish army than of famine!

The soldiers lost all hope. They hid in churches and houses. Bohemond burned down the buildings to force them out. But though the fire drove them to their posts it could not give them courage.

The knights were in despair. Tancred had promised never to leave the army while he had sixty men to follow him, but few were so brave as he was. The leaders gathered to speak of what could be done to save Antioch and the army from the Moslems. As they sat and talked, a monk named Peter Bartholemy stood before them. He had come so noiselessly that he startled them. He asked if he might speak. Then he told

HOW TANCRED FOUGHT

them that he had three times seen a vision of the apostle Andrew, and that he had said to him:

"At Antioch, in the Church of my brother St. Peter, the head of the lance that pierced the side of the Redeemer is hid near the high altar. In three days it will be shown to those who follow Him. Search, and ye shall find. Bear it high in battle, and the sacred weapon shall pierce the souls of the enemy."

For two days every one fasted. It was not difficult to fast in Antioch then. It was harder almost to eat the tasteless fragments that were all that could be found. On the third day men began to dig beside the altar in St. Peter's Church.

The diggers were weary, and those who watched them grew faithless or scornful, for though the hole grew deeper—six feet, nine feet, twelve feet—still no one had heard the clink of the lance-head against the spades. As evening fell, the monk Peter leapt barefoot into the hole. His spade sounded with a dull thud against the earth, but what was that? The digging ceased. Every one started and leant forward awe-struck. Peter clambered up and held a lance-head high in the air. They wrapt it in cloth of gold and purple, and all was stir in the army. The news of what had happened passed like flame from place to place. Men who had wished to die were eager and full of hope. The Crusaders were so sure that they would win, that they sent Peter the Hermit to the leader of the Moslems to offer to make peace with him. But he drove Peter the Hermit from him, and said that they had only to choose between slavery and death. He did not know how the

Peter held a lance-head high in the air.

thought of the sacred lance had roused the knights and their followers. When the trumpets sounded the call to arms he would scarcely leave the game of chess he was playing. It was no wonder that he scorned the army that came out to meet him. Most of the horses had died in Antioch. Knights rode from the city gates on camels and on asses. The foot soldiers were in rags, and some

HOW TANCRED FOUGHT

of them were lame. The Moslems had set fire to great heaps of hay round the city walls, and the famished army had to make its way through these. Hour passed after hour. It seemed as if even the courage of faith could not withstand the numbers of the Turks. But just then three wondrous knights in white and shining armour appeared. "The saints are coming to your aid." "St. George!" "St. George!" The shouts rang through the camp. The Crusaders rushed wildly on. The Saracens broke and fled. They were followed by Tancred and other brave knights until sunset.

The armies feasted again and lingered at Antioch, while the bolder knights longed and fretted to march for Jerusalem.

After many delays the Crusaders at length saw the Holy City rise in the distance. The sight of it brought out all that was best in them. Quarrels were forgotten. The Crusaders were not warriors now, they were pilgrims. Horsemen and foot-soldiers threw down their weapons and knelt on the rocky track. Many strong men wept as they rose and went towards the city in joy and awe.

A band of Christians from Bethlehem came to meet them and to plead with them not to forget the need of the village where Christ was born in their eagerness to rescue the town where He died. Tancred went with them, and a band of brave men followed him. He surprised the village at night, and the banner of the Cross waved over it in the morning sunshine. Then he rode back to join the army that marched towards Jerusalem. Before night fell again the Crusaders were

They knelt on the rocky track.

encamped before the Holy City. The soldiers were as eager to attack the city as the boldest of the knights. Although they had no engines that were strong enough and high enough to throw stones into the city, they tried to take it at once. They were driven back. But they were not hopeless, as they had often been before. They planned how they could best attack it again. To the south and east of Jerusalem the walls of the city rise from deep gorges. The Crusaders could not hope to build engines that would have power to shoot weapons and stones across these chasms. So they pitched their tents only to the north and to the west of the city, and laid siege to the walls from St. Stephen's gate at the

HOW TANCRED FOUGHT

north-east corner to the Tower of David at the south-west.

Then the knights looked for wood to make engines and platforms. They broke through the bands of Saracens who guarded the roads, and brought tools and food from ships that had come to Joppa, but still they looked in vain for trees large enough to make into battering rams and engines. One day Tancred and his men saw some trees in the distance. They looked large and strong, but he had so often hoped in vain to find what he wished, that he would scarcely let himself believe what his eyes saw. This time his hope was not in vain. When he reached the trees, he found that they were truly great forest trees, and though they were thirty miles from Jerusalem, he and his men soon cut down as many as were needed and dragged them to the camp.

All this time the sun had blazed down on the crusading army. In the heat and drought they dared not drink because the Moslems had poisoned the wells. But nothing could daunt their courage now, for the walls of the Holy City rose before them. The whole army fasted for three days. Then they marched round Jerusalem. Tancred and some other knights lingered on Mount Olivet, and thought of what had happened there hundreds of years ago. On the mountain there they were standing at about the same height as the walls of the city on the other side of the valley, and as they stood, they saw the Moslems mock them, by fixing crosses on the ramparts, and flinging mud at them to show how much they scorned the Christians and their worship.

As the knights came back to their camp the sun set and the Moslem call for prayer rang out from the minarets of the city. It was answered by the chant of the Crusaders, "So shall they fear the name of the Lord from the west, and His glory from the rising of the sun."

During the night the great engines were drawn close to the city wall. In the dim light of the morning, huge stones were shot into the city and showers of arrows fell within the walls.

The Saracens used dreadful weapons. They poured boiling oil on the Crusaders and set fire to their engines. The knights poured vinegar on the blazing towers of their engines to put out the flames, but soon they had emptied out every drop they had. Then they had to watch the platforms they had built with so much care fall in blazing ruins and crush the men on whom they fell. The battle raged all day. It opened again next morning, and again the fire of the Saracens burned the towers of the besiegers. It seemed as if the Crusaders must fail once more. But Godfrey saw the glistening armour of a knight on the mount of Olives. He shouted,

"It is St. George who has come again to help us."

The soldiers dashed once more to their engines. The wind changed and blew the flames into the city. That afternoon, Godfrey stood on the wall of Jerusalem. He and the knights who were with him hastened to St. Stephen's Gate and flung it open.

HOW TANCRED FOUGHT

"It is the will of God! It is the will of God," rang through the streets as the Moslems fled hither and thither for shelter.

Tancred rushed into the city. He saw before him the Mosque of Omar, and marked it for his own. When he entered it he found three hundred Moslems who had taken shelter there amongst the marble pillars. He promised to spare their lives and gave them a banner to prove that he meant to keep his word. But other Crusaders thought it very wrong of Tancred not to kill every Moslem, and, in spite of the banner, they slew all the men whom he had promised to save. The joy of the taking of Jerusalem was spoiled for Tancred. His honour had been set at nought. Still he did not cease to serve the cause he loved. He shared the treasure of the Mosque with Godfrey and with many of the soldiers who had fought with him. Then he gave what was over to build the Christian churches that lay in ruins.

The cross which had been thrown down and hidden was found. The knights set it up again in the Church of the Holy Sepulchre, and other thoughts than war and bloodshed filled the minds of the Crusaders. Godfrey flung aside his bloody sword and armour, clad himself in a robe of pure white linen, and with bare head and feet entered the ruined Church of the Holy Sepulchre. He knelt on the pavement and kissed the stone of the grave. One after another the knights followed him. Then the crowd turned to Peter the Hermit. They forgot that he had fled from Antioch. He was the hero of the day again as he had been in the market-places of the north.

The knights wished to choose a king. The choice lay between Tancred and Godfrey. But Tancred was a warrior; he did not wish to rule. Godfrey stood alone. The only thing that his servants could say against him was that he lingered too long in church, and cared not though they waited for him nor though his dinner grew cold.

Godfrey was chosen king, but when the crown was brought he refused to wear it. He said that he would never be crowned with gold where the Saviour of the world had worn the crown of thorns. Nor would he take the title of king. "Baron and Defender of the Holy Sepulchre," he called himself. But others called him Godfrey I., King of Jerusalem.

After this the Crusaders left him. Many of them went home to Europe; others scattered over the Holy Land.

Tancred, with three hundred knights and two thousand foot soldiers, stayed to defend the new kingdom. Godfrey reigned for less than a year. His death was a great sorrow to those who loved Jerusalem. Tancred lived for twelve years to fight the battles of the Holy City. He ruled Antioch while Bohemond was in prison, for he still was faithful to his cousin, though Bohemond's aims were low, his hopes selfish, and his heart cruel.

Tancred died in the strength of his manhood from a battle wound. In that rough time he was one

HOW TANCRED FOUGHT

"Than whom . . . is no nobler knight,
  More mild in manner, fair in manly bloom,
  Nor more sublimely daring in the fight."

CHAPTER III

HOW THE KINGS FOUGHT FOR GLORY AND NOT FOR CHRIST

After Godfrey died many kings reigned in Jerusalem, but amongst them all there was not one who was like him. The head of the Christian Church in the Holy Land was called the Patriarch of Jerusalem. There was great power in his hands, and often he and the king were enemies. Instead of trying to help one another to make the Christian power strong, they used each to try to get all the power away from the other. If it had not been for two great orders of knights, the Moslems would soon have swept the new kingdom away.

Long before the first Crusade, a hospice had been built near the Holy Sepulchre. The Brothers who lived there welcomed pilgrims and were kind to the poor. At the time of the taking of Jerusalem, they gave such ready help to the armies of the Cross that many crusading knights joined their brotherhood. These men promised always to fight against the Saracens and also to seek no wealth for themselves. They were called the Knights Hospitallers. They wore a long black robe with five white crosses on it in time of peace, but in time of war they wore an upper robe of red with a silver cross on its shoulder. The knights of the other order were named Templars. They wore a long white mantle with a red cross on the shoulder. In battle they carried a flag, half white and half black. It meant that they were simple and frank to Christians, but dark and fearsome to Moslems. The Templars were so proud of their vow of poverty that their seal was two knights on the back of one horse. But though they boasted of it they often forgot it in daily life.

If King and Patriarch, Hospitallers and Templars, had remembered that white-and-black banner, and had always been frank and simple to Christians, nothing could have stood against them. Instead of that, they often fought amongst themselves and said bitter things about each other, and weakened the kingdom they had vowed to strengthen.

In Europe there had been many changes. The Crusade had done far less for the Christians in the Holy Land than Peter had dreamed it would do. But it had done much for the countries to which the Crusaders belonged. It had made people think for themselves.

But every one did not think that that was a good thing. Bernard, who preached the second Crusade, did not think so. He wished the power of the Church to rule everything and every one. He was a very great man, and while he lived kings and emperors obeyed him, as if they had been little children. The Pope himself used to ask him to tell him what he must do. Bernard always knew what he wished, and he quickly found the best way to gain his ends, for his heart was simple, and he coveted no earthly honour nor wealth for himself. He had become a monk when he was very young. Though he had been brought up in great comfort, he only ate coarse bread soaked in warm water. He was as unwilling to give pleasure to his mind as to his body. One time some friends came to see him and made him smile. He thought this was a great sin, and he lay before the altar for twenty-five days praying for pardon.

When any one wished to enter his order, he said to them, "You must leave your body outside, only spirits can enter here."

Yet though Bernard was a great and strong man, the Crusade he planned ended in failure. Thousands of knights and soldiers died in Asia, and the leaders came back to Europe with only a handful of the men who had followed them in the wars.

Not very long after the return of these fighting men, a lad named Saladin went to Egypt from Damascus. Saladin liked pleasure and idleness, and he was very unwilling to leave his happy home in the north to go to Egypt to fight under his uncle. When he was told that he must do this, he said, "I go, but with the despair of a man led to death." The ruler of Egypt had many men around him who wished for more power and honour than they had, and he was afraid that one of them would kill him and take his place. He saw Saladin, and noticed that he seemed careless about making a name for himself, and yet that he was a very great fighter when he was roused by battle. This made him wish to have him always with him, and so Saladin was made ruler of the forces.

HOW THE KINGS FOUGHT FOR GLORY

But then a strange change came over Saladin. He no sooner had charge of men than he ceased to be a thoughtless lad, and became a serious leader of armies. Instead of growing slowly, as most people do, he seemed to change all at once from a playful, self-willed child to a strong man, who could bear all hardships to gain his end. Soon the ruler of Egypt died, and Saladin reigned in his place. Ere long he was Lord of Bagdad too, and that meant that he had power over the whole Moslem world.

During all this time the kings of Jerusalem were weak, powerless men. At first Saladin wished to make a truce with the one who reigned when he became Lord of Bagdad. This was not because he had any kind feeling towards him. He only wished to get time to make his own kingdom strong ere he fought for the little belt of Syrian land that belonged to the Christians. It was the only bit in all that part of the world that he did not rule.

But a noble of the kingdom of Jerusalem, named the Lord of Carac, broke the truce. He robbed caravans and killed Moslems whenever he could. Saladin was very angry. He could wait no longer, but decided to fight for Jerusalem at once.

In the Holy City, jealousy and bitterness were making strife amongst those who ought to have been friends. Red cross knights hated white cross knights. When they did uphold each other it was not in order to fight the foe, but to fight the priests. They even shot arrows at them in the streets of Jerusalem. The priests gathered up the arrows, laid them out under the open sky, and prayed that God would punish the knights. And when the time came to face Saladin, it was not possible to get the Christian army to fight as one man.

The Saracens took the town of Tiberias on the Lake of Galilee. The news of this was brought to the King of Jerusalem as he rode out to meet Saladin. Count Raymond, in whose land Tiberias was, rode beside the king. The Count's wife and children were in the town, but yet Raymond said:

"This army is all we have: if we lose it, the Holy City will be lost. Let us go to some place where Saladin will have to attack us, where we shall hold the fortress instead of attacking him. I would rather lose this country and all that I possess, if by that I might save the Holy City."

But the other knights made the king believe that Raymond said this because he was really on Saladin's side, and wished him to win. The king yielded to them, and the army marched forward to Tiberias. When they reached the town, they found that all the heights on the hills round it were fortified. For two days a terrible battle raged. The Moslems even were astonished at the brave way the crusading army fought to save the wood of the true Cross which they had carried into the fight. They said that "the knights flew round it like moths round a candle."

But at last the bishop who bore it was killed, and the Cross was carried to Saladin's camp. When the Crusaders raised the body of the dead bishop they found that he had worn a coat of mail under his robe, and they thought that it was because of his want of faith

HOW THE KINGS FOUGHT FOR GLORY

that they had lost the battle, for always before, the bearer of the Cross had gone unarmed into battle.

When the Cross was taken, the crusading army lost all courage. One after another of the leaders was taken prisoner. Count Raymond escaped, but soon he died of misery for a lost cause and a lost home.

When the king and the Lord of Carac were brought before Saladin the Moslem welcomed the king kindly. He offered him a great goblet full of cool wine. The king was hot and faint from battle. The wine was pleasant to him, and it made him hope for kindness from Saladin.

The king drank. Then he passed the goblet to the Lord of Carac, but Saladin seized his arm

"That traitor shall not drink in my presence," he shouted.

The count looked at him with scorn, and made his rage hotter by acting as boldly as if he had been a free man in his own castle.

"Choose between the Moslem faith and death!" said Saladin. Carac had not been true to the truce, but he would not give up his loyalty to the Crusaders in order to save his life. Quick as thought the scimitar of a Turkish soldier severed the head of the count from his body, which fell lifeless at the feet of the king. Then the captive knights were led in.

"Slay every one his man. I will rid the earth of these unclean races," said Saladin to his warriors. They hung back. The knights were prisoners of war and unarmed, and the Moslem soldiers did not wish to butcher them. But Saladin would not listen even to his own soldiers when they asked him to spare his captives. They had to do his will, and knight after knight fell dead before the king.

After these terrible days Saladin went with haste to Jerusalem. He sent this message to the Christians in the city:

"I, as well as you, count Jerusalem to be the house of God; I will not defile it with blood if I can gain it by peace and love. Give it up, and I will give you freedom to go where you will, and as much land as you can till."

But they answered:

"We cannot yield the city in which our God died. Still less can we sell it to you."

By and by, when they saw that they could not hold out against Saladin, they offered to agree to what he had said.

"It is too late," replied Saladin; "look at my yellow banners floating from the wall!" He did not know how brave the men were. When they heard his answer they sent this message:

"Very well, we will destroy the city. Your mosque and the stone of Jacob which you worship shall be made into dust. Five thousand Moslem prisoners shall be slain. Then we will kill our wives and our children, and march out to you with fire and sword. Not one of us will die till ten Moslems lie slain by his sword."

HOW THE KINGS FOUGHT FOR GLORY

When Saladin heard these threats, he said he would let each citizen who could pay for his ransom go free.

On the day on which the Christians were to leave Jerusalem, Saladin sat on a throne and watched the stream of people press out of the gate. First came the priests. They bore the Communion vessels and the ornaments of the Church of the Holy Sepulchre. Then the queen came, and with her a band of nobles, and then the great crowd of people. They were very sad. They were leaving their homes and their city, and some of them were leaving friends for whom no ransom money could be found. Now and again the line was broken and some one took courage to fall before the Sultan to beg for the freedom of husband or of children who had been left behind. Saladin and his brother paid the ransom money for thousands, and only a small band stayed to be the slaves of the Moslems.

The saddened Christians were gone from the streets of the Holy City, and a crowd of joyous and excited people surged everywhere. Jerusalem was nearly as sacred to the Moslems as to those they had conquered. They hurled down a great cross from the dome above which it stood. They washed the mosque of Omar within and without with rosewater, that no Christian dust even might lie on the walls or floors. Allah is the name by which Moslems speak of God, and Saladin was welcomed everywhere as "the bright star of Allah."

When the news of the fall of Jerusalem reached Europe, the grief was terrible. The Pope died of sorrow.

The royal courts went into mourning. The priests veiled the statues in the churches. Songs of love and chivalry were forgotten, and the minstrels sang only of the captured city.

Three great kings vowed to regain the Holy City. They were King Richard of England, King Philip of France, and the Emperor Frederick of Germany. The emperor was the first to set out. He is called "Barbarossa," because that means "red beard," and he had a great red beard. He had an army of strong warriors. His men loved him, and they did what he bade them without a murmur. He never allowed them to idle away their time or to grow soft and lazy after a victory, but swept them on in perfect order from battle to battle and carried all before him. The news of his great march came to Saladin, and even he feared lest his armies might not be able to face so great a band of warriors. But one day as Frederick rested on the banks of a river that flowed through the country north of the Holy Land, he longed to bathe in the cool stream. He plunged in, but something stunned him, and the great Emperor Barbarossa was drawn up on the bank only to die. He was buried in the Crusader Church at Tyre. But his people in Germany could not believe that he was dead. They made this beautiful legend about him. They said he had been borne from the East by magic, and that he lies in a great hall in Germany and waits there until his country needs him. When her need is greatest he will waken, they say, and burst the doors of his prison and come to save her. But no one has seen the red glow of Barbarossa's beard in the dimly lighted hall, nor has any one found the castle in which he lies.

HOW THE KINGS FOUGHT FOR GLORY

Barbarossa waits until his country needs him.

Many soldiers in France and England grew weary of waiting for their kings, and hastened to fight under the banner of the King of Jerusalem.

When at length King Philip and King Richard set out, they were stayed by a storm at an island on their way to the Holy Land. They spent the winter there, but they lost much more than time. For years they had been friends, but now that they had set out on the same quest, they quarrelled so fiercely, that though they both did many brave deeds, all were marred by the bitter hatred and jealousy that had sprung up between them.

When Philip reached the Christian armies, he found that they were laying siege to Acre. They were in great danger. Their camp lay round the landward walls of the city. But beyond their tents lay the Moslem camp, and when the knights attacked Acre, bands of their foes could rush on the camp and destroy those who were left to guard it. The sails of Philip's fleet were seen with joy by the crusading army, but when he landed he said he would not fight till Richard came. Even when at length both kings were in the camp, the whole force would not fight together. Richard was so much afraid that Philip's army would be praised for what the English knights had done, and Philip was so much afraid that England would be praised for the brave deeds of the French, that when the one king fought, the other looked on!

Sometimes days and even weeks passed with no fighting. And during those times of peace, the two Christian kings were more friendly with Saladin than they were with each other. Once they both lay ill. Each of them thought that perhaps the other had sent poison to him and caused his illness, but they both took food and doctors from Saladin without fear. In times of peace too, the warriors from the Moslem camp and the crusading knights held tournaments and dances in the open spaces between the tents. And even in battle, signs of the strange friendship were seen, for Saladin rode into the fight with the badge of chivalry on his breast.

The common soldiers did not know what to think. They had come with their lords to fight for the Holy City and to help Christians who were in misery, and their masters seemed far more eager to give gifts to the Moslem leaders and to do great deeds of daring than to take Jerusalem.

HOW THE KINGS FOUGHT FOR GLORY

But though Richard and Philip forgot to fight only for the relief of Christians, Saladin did not forget that he meant to rid the land of Christians. He admired the brave deeds of Richard, but he meant to drive Richard from his land.

After two years, Acre fell into the hands of the crusading armies. The knights wished to make Saladin promise to give back the wood of the true cross. Those who really cared about winning the land back for the kingdom of Jerusalem, thought that the loss of this precious relic had been the cause of all their trouble. People believed very queer things in those days, and one of the things they believed was that all over Europe, since the wood of the true cross had been taken from the bishop at Tiberias, babies had only had twenty-two teeth instead of thirty-two. But Richard himself did not care very much about the wood of the true cross, so he let the Moslems keep it.

Saladin was very angry when other people did not keep their promises, but he was in no haste to pay the ransom he had said he would give if those who lived in Acre were set free. Richard was so angry at the delay that he slew five thousand prisoners. Philip was longing to go back to France, and he made this cruel act of Richard's his excuse. About this time Richard offended two other warriors. He vexed a noble called Conrade, and he tore down the standard of Leopold of Austria. Philip sailed away, and the other two nobles allowed Richard to stand alone as the leader of the crusading army, but they never forgot his pride and wilfulness.

As he led his forces south towards Jerusalem a host of Saracens met them. There seemed no hope of victory or even of safety, but the thought that the Holy City was near, made the Crusaders fight with all their might, and the foe fled before them. While they were rejoicing in this, another Moslem army swept down on them and all seemed lost, when Richard galloped to the head of his men, and once more the Christians won the field.

Though King Richard was a great warrior, and though sometimes the thought of Jerusalem made him wish nothing so much as that he might win it from the Saracens, he did not always care to be true to his vows. After this victory he made a gay court for himself at a town called Joppa. He rode out to hunt and to seek adventures. Sometimes he was nearly killed. Once he was in the midst of a band of Saracens. They were going to make him prisoner when a French knight who was with him, shouted:

"Spare me! I am the king!"

He only said that to let the king go free. The Saracens rushed at the knight, and the king rode off safely.

Another time Richard saw the enemy come down and attack a small band of knights who had ridden out to seek food for their horses. He saw that they were in danger, and he leapt on to his horse and galloped across the plain. Those who had been with him hastened to follow him, but when they saw how many Saracens there were, they begged him to turn and leave the

HOW THE KINGS FOUGHT FOR GLORY

knights to be taken. He was full of anger and, turning to them, he said:

"How could I ever bear the name of king again if I left my followers to die without help."

He rushed at the foe. The knights, who had been taken by surprise, felt new courage rise when they saw the king. He and they slashed right and left with their swords, and ere long Richard led the whole party joyously back to the camp at Joppa.

While the Crusaders lived in this gay court, the Christians at Jerusalem, whom they had vowed to help, were hard at work building walls and fortresses, for Saladin wished to make Jerusalem so strong that even Richard could not take it, so he made the Christians who were in his power build the walls that were to keep their friends from helping them.

After feasting at Joppa, Richard led his army to Ascalon. He hoped to capture the town and all the great forts that had been built there, for Ascalon was one of the strongest fortresses in the land. When the army came near the town, the faces of the leaders fell, for Ascalon was only a heap of ruins. Saladin could not spare men to defend it, and instead of trying to hold it he made his men pull down stone from stone, that no one else might find safety within it. It grieved him to do this, and he said that he would rather that one of his sons had died than that the fortress should be thrown down. But he was not like Richard, who sometimes wished one thing and sometimes another. He wished only one thing, and that was that every crusading knight should either die or leave the Holy Land. So though it hurt him to destroy the strong towers and walls of Ascalon, he did it.

When Richard saw the ruins, he cast aside his armour, and set himself to heave the great stones from the heaps where they lay, and to build them again into defences. Knights and soldiers did as they saw their leader do, and soon the walls began to rise again. For a short time all went well, but then some of the nobles grew weary of such heavy work when it had none of the glamour of war to make up for the hardship. The first to throw down his building tools was Leopold, whose banner Richard had torn down at Acre. He turned away with anger, and said:

"I am not a carpenter nor yet a mason."

Others did as he had done, and looked on with scorn on those who still worked with Richard. Even amongst those who were not idle there were many who longed to hasten on to Jerusalem. They knew that even the great Saladin feared to meet Richard with his armies. The courage of the English king was as highly thought of in the Saracen camp as in his own. It was said that the manes of the Arab horses bristled when Richard's name was spoken, and that, if a rider in the Holy Land felt his horse start beneath him, he would say:

"Dost see King Richard in that bush?"

It was no wonder that the armies, who had suffered so much to win the Holy City, should grieve that Richard would not march upon it. At last he yielded to their wishes, and he and his knights swept across the country towards Jerusalem. All was joyous and cheerful. The heralds shouted the old call, "Save the Holy

HOW THE KINGS FOUGHT FOR GLORY

Sepulchre!" and it seemed as if once more the Banner of the Cross would wave over the city where Christ died. Saladin withdrew into the city. Each new messenger told of the fear and dread that was in the Saracen camp, and the army of the Cross marched forward with high hopes.

But amongst those who were nearest to Richard, there were some who urged him to turn back. They said that even if Jerusalem were taken by them they could not hold it. Richard listened to them. He wavered. His army looked eagerly towards the city whose towers and domes rose dimly into sight in the distance. He gave one longing look, and turned his back on Jerusalem.

But though Richard turned away towards the sea, he was scarcely less vexed than his army. He was more enraged against the Saracens than he had ever been, and from this time onward he fought with even more reckless courage than before. He took ship from Acre and sailed along the coast to Joppa. But ere his ships entered the harbour, the Saracens seized the town. Richard could not wait till his vessel reached the harbour. He plunged into the water, landed, and rushed at the enemy with his brave knights close behind him. The Saracens fled. Within three days they came back, and Richard was roused from his sleep by the cry,

"To arms!"

There was no time to put on armour. There was scarcely time even to dress. As Richard sprang into the saddle, he shouted:

"Fight like men whose only hope is in courage. Verily, I myself shall sever the head of him who fails in his duty."

The great host of the Saracens rushed on. Trumpets pealed, and banners streamed in the air. There seemed no hope for the small band of knights. But the lion-hearted king was with the knights, and victory followed his sword. Men could scarcely believe that he was human, for wherever the battle was hottest Richard seemed to spring from the ground. Once it seemed as if he were lost among the Saracens. Fear filled the hearts of his men, when suddenly Richard rode towards them from the ranks of the foe. He was mounted on a horse they had not seen before. His own had fallen under him, and the brother of Saladin had sent two to him in the midst of the battle, because he thought him so brave and so great a warrior that he could not bear to see him fight on foot. The Crusaders won the day, but as they returned to the camp they found another battle before them. The foe had entered the city. The day had been long and hard, but the spirit of the knights was strong and fearless, and soon they were masters of Joppa again. When all was over they gazed at each other. It did not seem possible even to themselves that they had won so great a victory. Hundreds of Saracens lay dead on the plain and only one knight had fallen.

But Richard was eager to return to England. He wished to make peace. Saladin did not wish for peace. He wished to sweep every Christian from his land. But his officers thought that if Richard would only leave the land they would not fear the other Crusaders, and they

HOW THE KINGS FOUGHT FOR GLORY

thought he would go at once if Saladin made peace with him. When the peace was made, it was agreed that many seaport towns should belong to the Christians, and that all might go to Jerusalem to visit the holy places there. In order that the promises that were made might be as sacred to one side as to the other, they were made in presence of the Bible and of the Koran, for the Koran was as holy to the Saracens as the Bible was to the Christian army.

Richard had been eager to make peace, but when the moment came when he had to leave the Holy Land, it seemed as if his heart would break. Although there were some in the army who did not trust him, and some who envied him, there were many hundreds who loved him so much that they did not care to serve under any other leader. They gathered round him weeping, and watched him step on to the vessel. As the king looked back over the land he had hoped to win, he said:

"O Holy Land! God bless thy people and grant that I may come again to visit and help thee!"

Richard did not care to go through France on his way home, because he had made Philip so bitter an enemy. He tried to make his way across Europe further west and north. Sometimes he dressed as a pilgrim, sometimes as a merchant. But he had been too long a great king to find it easy to act like any one else.

In one place he had to ask a count to allow him to pass from one land to another. He called himself the merchant Hugo, and sent a squire to ask for leave to go on. He told him to offer a costly ruby ring to the count to whom he was sent. But the count was a friend of one of Richard's foes. He had heard much about the wars, and he at once thought that this great ruby ring could only belong to the King of England. He sent back the ring with a kind message, but though he promised to do as he had been asked, he laid plans to capture the merchant Hugo! Richard escaped as a pilgrim, but even after that he would not be wise, for even in a pilgrim's dress he went on wearing a great ring on his finger, and he let his squire go to market-places with a purse full of coins that came from the Holy Land. The lad boasted of them, and showed them to those who gathered round him. Then, when it was too late, he saw what he had done and ran to warn his master, but Richard would not flee. He was taken prisoner by Leopold, whose banner he had torn down from the walls of Acre, and who had been the first to throw away his building tools at Ascalon.

The people of England longed to see him. They had heard how brave he had been in battle. They loved the thought of him, but what could they do to save him? They did not know where he was. The story of the way in which they found out is a strange one. Before the king went to the Holy Land, he and his minstrel Blondel had made a little song which they sang verse about. Blondel loved Richard greatly, and he set out to search for him. He asked where Richard had last been seen. Then he went from village to village. If a castle stood in sight, he asked if any prisoner lay there. If there was one, he tried to find out what kind of a man he was. Once he was in great excitement. The villagers near a castle told him of a prisoner who seemed to be a man like King Richard. But Blondel wished to be certain that

HOW THE KINGS FOUGHT FOR GLORY

he was right before he went back to England. When he was sure that no one saw him he ran to the castle. He looked at all sides of it till he thought he knew where the dungeon was. Then he sang some lines of the old song. His voice was broken and shaky, and when he stopped and waited he could scarcely breathe, he was so eager to know if anything would happen. Something did happen. Richard's voice from within the castle carried on the song.

When Blondel reached England and told where the king lay a prisoner, he soon roused the people to give a great sum of money in return for his freedom.

Before Richard had landed in England, Saladin lay dead. As the Christian pilgrims longed to go to Jerusalem, so he had longed to go to Mecca, for that is the holiest city in the world to those who follow the prophet. But Saladin was too ill to go to Mecca. When he lay dying in Damascus, he sent his heralds out to go through the streets of the city. As they marched, no banners were to stream behind them. Instead of a banner the shroud he was soon to need was borne along beside them, while they shouted as he bade them:

"This, this is all that remains of the glory of Saladin who conquered the East!"

CHAPTER IV

HOW FREDERICK CAME TO HIS KINGDOM

The kingdom of Jerusalem was in dire need of help. But all the powerful people in Europe were busy fighting with each other. Once the thought of the Crusades had been enough to stir every heart, now the great wars had become the games of children. In the villages, children played at sieges and battles. The priests still longed to see the Holy City the centre of a strong kingdom. They spoke to kings and nobles, and pled with them to go forth bravely as others had done to win renown in wars of the Cross. But no one heeded them. They watched the children playing at war, and the thought came that if the men would not go, the children might. It was many years since Richard and Philip had set forth, and men had a little forgotten how hard the way was. Besides, some people thought that if children left their homes and all the ease of life to fight in a holy war, God would give them the strength of men, and would make everything easy before them. So when the warriors would not listen, the priests preached to the children. They told them that a dry pathway would be made through the great sea, and that the children would have the strength of heaven in their arms. And the children listened and followed the preachers. Here and there a lad knew what the priest meant and believed what he said, and caught sight of the grand dream that had made Tancred and Godfrey leave all for Jerusalem so long before. But most of the children knew but little of what they wished or of what a Crusade meant. They had played at battles till they liked nothing else so much, and now they ran and danced along through the villages of Europe as merrily as if they had only been going to see a fair in the nearest town. Mothers and fathers pled with them to stay. They tried to keep them back by force. But they had only one answer:

"To Jerusalem."

When they reached the shore, the waves on the beach broke against their feet quietly and steadily. No path opened before them. Those who tried to wade in soon scrambled back to land. They had neither money nor food. They were a sorrowful band, and kind people in Italy drew those who would come into their homes, and allowed them to grow up amongst their own children. But there were many who would neither go back to their own lands nor stay in Italy. They wandered by the shore and dreamed of the Holy City. Then they heard of ships that were to sail to the south. The captains offered to take the little Crusaders to the Holy Land without payment. The children crowded on to the vessels, and thought that now at last they were on the way to save Jerusalem. But ere many days had gone by they looked at each other with sad and frightened faces. The captains were wicked, cruel men, and the little children were sold as slaves.

Though the children fought no battle, the story of their sorrows roused Europe to a new Crusade. This time the armies tried to reach Jerusalem from the South. They landed in Egypt at the mouth of the Nile, and took the town of Damietta. But they were not strong enough to drive the enemy away from their camp beside the city. Every day the two forces fought with each other. Besides those who fell in battle, hundreds of warriors were drowned in the Nile. In each camp envy and spite were dividing those who ought to have thought only of the cause for which they fought. Into the midst of all this hatred a strange figure came. It was the figure of St. Francis. He was very unlike all others in the crusading camp, for he did not come to fight, but only to help and to love. He nursed the sick and wounded by day and by night, and as he went from tent to tent the rough soldiers looked at him with awe. His body was worn and spent, yet he never showed that he was tired. It seemed as if he could make himself do whatever he willed to do, even when it was something that men thought impossible.

As he went through the camp, he often looked across to the Saracen tents.

"If they only knew," he thought.

He wished to tell them about Jesus Christ. He did not think that any one who knew about Him could do anything but love and serve Him. The longing to tell them grew so strong that he could not stay. He went alone to the enemies' camp and entered the sultan's tent. He told him of Jesus Christ and of the Christian faith, but the sultan listened carelessly. He was not

HOW FREDERICK CAME TO HIS KINGDOM

moved by the passionate words of St. Francis, who grew more and more eager.

"Test what I say by fire," he said. "Choose the most faithful follower of your prophet, and he and I will walk through fire together. Then you will know that the one whom the flames do not hurt is the one that God owns."

The sultan looked at him. He thought that the Christian monk was mad. He would not hear of sending one of his men to walk through fire. But Francis tried once more to win his Church's enemy.

"I will pass alone through the fire," he said, "if you will promise to worship Christ if I am not burned."

The sultan would not promise, and the Saracen soldiers shouted, "Behead him, behead him!"

But the sultan was not angry with him. He liked him because of his courage, and though he would not do what Francis wished, he offered him many costly gifts. Francis would not take one. They had no charm for him. He had vowed to be poor all his life.

He was very sad as he left the camp. He had been so eager to win the Saracens by love, to believe in Christ, and they would not even think of what he said to them.

All who joined this Crusade were not like Francis in their thoughts and wishes. Frederick, Emperor of Germany and King of Italy, was very unlike the gentle monk. He had married the daughter of the Queen of Jerusalem, and called himself King of Jerusalem, although his father-in-law was still alive. He wished to reign over the Holy Land, but he liked the ease of his court too well to be in haste to fight. He had friends, too, amongst the Saracens, so though the Pope bade him set forth on the Crusade, he always found an excuse for delay. At last he did sail, but he became ill and landed again in three days.

The Pope was so angry that he preached against him. He said that the illness was not real.

The clergy and the Pope stood round the altar in the great cathedral at Rome. The bells clanged above. Each man except the Pope carried a lighted torch. After the Pope had spoken of all the wrong things the emperor had done he paused. Then in the dim light he prayed that God would curse Frederick. As he prayed, the clergy lowered the torches and dashed out their flames against the stone floor to show the darkness in which they wished that Frederick's soul might be.

All this was told to Frederick. He was terribly angry. He had not cared much about the Crusade before, but now that the Pope had cursed him, he made up his mind that come what might he would reign in Jerusalem.

He set sail once more, but while he went slowly with his heavy war ships towards Acre, a swift ship passed his fleet. It reached the Holy Land long before he did, and two monks who had sailed in it, and who had been sent by the Pope, raised the Christians against him. When he landed, no welcome waited him, though he had come to fight for the kingdom of Jerusalem against the Saracens. Although the knights would not serve under him, yet nothing could daunt him. He had

HOW FREDERICK CAME TO HIS KINGDOM

learned the language of the Saracens, so when the Christians would not own him he planned a treaty with their foes. The sultan promised to give up Bethlehem, Nazareth, and the whole of the city of Jerusalem except the part where the mosque of the prophet had stood for ten years. But though this pleased the sultan and Frederick, it did not please any one else. The Saracens were angry that the Holy City had been given to the Crusaders. The Pope and the Christians were angry that the worship of the prophet should have any place within Jerusalem. The Pope was still more enraged to think that the man that he had cursed would be king in Jerusalem.

For years the Pope had been urging his people to go on pilgrimage to Jerusalem. Many had hastened to the Holy Land, and thought gladly now that they could do as they had vowed, but the Pope sent messages from Rome that no one who cared for his wishes was even to pray at the Holy Sepulchre.

Frederick entered Jerusalem. He passed through empty streets, for priests and men and women fled from him.

He marched to the Church of the Holy Sepulchre followed by a small band of his warriors. He entered the empty church. He saw that the images of the apostles were veiled, and that no priest stood by the altar. No sound of music or of song rose on the air. Only the armour of the soldiers clanked on the pavement, and the step of Frederick rang hard and sharp as he strode to the altar.

He lifted the crown that lay there and placed it on his head, but none save the handful of knights who followed him owned him King of Jerusalem.

Frederick did not long enjoy even this empty title of king. He went back to Europe, and ere long Jerusalem was taken by other victors than either sultan or emperor.

CHAPTER V

HOW LOUIS THOUGHT DEATH A LITTLE THING

Before the first Crusade, the Turks had poured westward to Palestine. Now before the last Crusade, another wild and fierce race swept down from China on Europe. They were called Tartars, and the terror of them spread to far countries. Villagers in France and Italy pointed to curious clouds in the sky, and turned pale; they thought them a sign that the monsters called Tartars were coming. Men and women cowered away in terror at the sight of a forest fire; they thought the Tartars had kindled it.

Such a tribe swept over the Holy Land and Moslem and Christian joined together to fight the terrible foe. But even though they fought side by side, they could not turn the fierce warriors back. On and on they came till their horses dashed up the streets of Jerusalem. The city was empty. Every one had fled. But the victors were cruel men, they wished to kill their foes as well as to take the city. They flung the banner of the cross out against the sky, and rang glad peals on the

STORIES FROM THE CRUSADES

A wild and fierce race called Tartars

bells of the Christian churches. In the caves and amongst the rocks round Jerusalem hundreds of people were hiding. They heard the bells, and peered out to see what had happened. They saw no foeman's flag, but their own banner waving. The news spread from rock to rock and from cave to cave. Crowds of joyful people hurried back to their city and to their homes. But the pealing bells and the floating banners drew them on only to death. The enemy waited till all were either within the gates or close to them. Then they fell on them and killed them.

HOW LOUIS THOUGHT DEATH A LITTLE THING

At this time King Louis of France was a young man of twenty-six. His father had died when he was ten. Since that time, his mother, Queen Blanche, had guarded his lands and had trained him to be a good and true man. She was a wise woman, and strong and beautiful. She was kind too, and she charmed those whom she ruled.

Louis was a handsome young king, fair and slight. His long hair flowed over his shoulders. He did not care to wear gay clothes, for he was prouder of the coarse hair shirt which he wore under his armour than of all his royal robes. To all who met him, he was gentle and courteous.

Once he was very ill. His nobles stood round his bed. They thought he was dead. Suddenly he spoke in a hollow voice. He bade the Bishop of Paris fasten the cross of the Holy War on his shoulder.

When he was well again many of his people wished him to stay in France and rule them, for Louis thought of many things that would help the people of his land. He made good laws, and he was just and kind. Those who wished him to stay at home said that he need not keep the promise he had made to go to fight in Palestine, because he was so ill when he made it that perhaps he did not know what he said. When this was said to Louis, the Bishop of Paris chanced to be beside him again. The king snatched the cross from his shoulder and gave it to the bishop. Then he said:

"Now at least, I am in my senses, and I vow that no food shall enter my lips till the cross is again on my shoulder."

So they knew that they need not urge him again to stay.

It was Christmas Eve. The king sat in a dimly lighted hall. The nobles of the court were called to him that he might fulfil an old French custom of mantle-giving. It was an honour to be called, and each man went up gladly to the king and felt a thrill of pleasure as the folds of the mantle fell from his shoulders. The nobles went from the king's presence into the chapel for the Christmas Eve service. As the bright light fell on the new cloaks, the knights started in surprise. The Cross of the Holy War had been fastened to each mantle. Each man saw it on his neighbour. Then he looked at his own robe and saw it there. Some smiled; some shrank from the vow; but the king's will was law, and his nobles made ready to sail.

In this crusade there were no gay robes nor jewelled bridles. Nor were there any ragged camp followers. Louis's army was made up of strong workmen and nobles.

The wild warrior tribe that had so cruelly killed the people of Jerusalem had left the land again and once more the Holy City was in the hands of the Sultan of Egypt. Louis hoped to surprise him and to attack him at the mouth of the Nile, but the Egyptian heard that he was coming and was ready to meet him. He brought a fleet of ships down the Nile and he lined the shores with armies.

When the two fleets met, the ships spread over miles of water. Close to the shore the fleet of Egypt lay. In a half-circle round it the crusading vessels gleamed in

HOW LOUIS THOUGHT DEATH A LITTLE THING

the sunshine, and the banner of the Cross waved from each topmast. Away out to sea one ship lay alone. From it, Queen Marguerite, the wife of Louis, watched the battle.

In the morning, the knights who were to fight on shore led their horses on planks from the great warships to the barges that lay alongside. The horses lurched and plunged in the unsteady boats, and the clang of their armour rang out across the water. All was noise and clamour. Hundreds of rowers bent to the oars. The barges bounded forward. Suddenly the sunlight was darkened. Spears and arrows from the Egyptian army flew so thick around the Crusaders that they could not see the sky. The rowers flagged. But the voice of Louis

Louis sprang into the water.

rang out to cheer them, and they bent to the oars with greater strength than ever. As the boat that bore the king touched the ground, Louis leapt into the water though it reached to his shoulder, and dashed through it sword in hand. Nobles and men followed him. The army that lined the shore broke its ranks and fled. But almost before the Crusaders could form in line, the horse soldiers of the Moslem army swept down on them from the desert.

Louis was so calm that he knelt for a moment on the sand. "Thy will be done!" he murmured. Then he sprang up and rushed into the fight. As the day wore on, Queen Marguerite as she watched, saw the oriflamme of France push slowly up the beach. Ship after ship that had guarded the river mouth sank. They were pierced by the prows of the French vessels. Ere night the victory was won. The crusading camp rang with shouts of joy.

In the morning a blaze of fire was seen in the south. Damietta, the town that Louis hoped to take for his own, was in flames. The foe had burned the city. No riches were left to tempt the army, so the burning of the city both helped and hindered Louis. Queen Marguerite landed and formed her court within the charred and ruined walls of Damietta. The army waited for more ships and men. But while they waited, bands of Arabs came whirling down on the camp. They came to any part of it that seemed less guarded, entered the tents, killed those they found there, and carried off the heads of all they killed. These wild men took the heads of the Crusaders to the sultan, who gave a golden coin for each one. Their horses were so swift and light that they

HOW LOUIS THOUGHT DEATH A LITTLE THING

could always escape from the heavy chargers of the knights. While the troops led by Louis were waiting here, the sultan was busy. The town of Mansourah stands at the place where the great river Nile breaks into many channels and forms the delta at its mouth. There the Moslem leader made ready to fight the French king. He built walls and towers, and made the town strong against the armies of the Cross.

At last the Crusaders marched, but when they reached Mansourah they found a great stream of water between them and the city. They could not fight the foe until they had crossed the channel. Then Louis bade his men build a causeway across the stream. But even as they built, the enemy on the other side dug away the sandy bank, and the stream flowed on as broad as before.

A shout was heard "A ford, a ford." It was not a good ford that had been found, still it was possible to cross by it, and the eager armies hastened to it. Robert, the king's brother, begged to be allowed to cross first with his men. He said he would wait on the other bank and guard the ford till the rest of the army had crossed over. A band of Moslems tried to keep him from landing. He drove them back. They fled across the sand.

Then Robert forgot his promise to stay by the ford. The masters of the knights of Jerusalem who rode with him begged him to think. They knew that it was a great mistake to break away from the other warriors. But Robert was too eager to listen. He said bitter things to them and seemed to think that they wished to keep all the power in their own hands. They were very angry at this, and the master of the Templars, to show that he was neither a coward nor wilful, shouted out:

"Raise then the standard."

But William Longsword of England still tried to keep Robert from his folly.

"What cowards these English are!" said Robert.

But Longsword was no coward. Robert had his way. He swept on with his followers, and chased the Moslems into their fortress of Mansourah. But it was only one part of the Moslem army that he defeated. Bibars, a Saracen leader, saw what had happened. He gathered his forces, and ere Robert knew what was going on, his foes were at Mansourah, shutting it in on every side, and he and his men were prisoners in the town they had won. They fought all day long. Very few of them lived to see the next morning's sun. William Longsword, whom Robert had called a coward, fought so bravely that even his foes noted where he fell, and after the fight was over gave back his body to his friends.

But long ere nightfall, Louis had crossed the ford with the other part of the crusading army. Instead of comrades waiting to guard their landing, they found only the track of fighting, and foes on every side. They broke into bands. Instead of one great attack a hundred battles were fought. The orders Louis gave could not be heard, for his voice was drowned in the noise and clamour of armour and of hoofs. No one knew what to do next. It seemed that all must be lost.

HOW LOUIS THOUGHT DEATH A LITTLE THING

Then Louis dashed forward with a small bodyguard. His haste was so great that he left his guard behind him, and found himself alone in the midst of six Moslem warriors. They knew he was the king by his armour. It seemed as if he must yield. But Louis was a great fighter, and he did not know what fear was. He held the six at bay until his guards joined him; then with them he led his army on in one wild charge, and won the day. But though they were victors they had suffered so greatly that it would have been wise if they had gone back to Damietta. This they would not do. They camped by the battle-field, and there very many of them grew ill and died. There was little food, and the air was evil-smelling and deadly. Louis went in and out amongst his men. As a nurse to them he was as tender and patient as he had been bold and fearless in war. At length he too fell ill.

He knew that something must be done to make peace with the sultan, for no help could come to Jerusalem from a host of Christian soldiers who were dying on the sands of Egypt. So he sent a message to say he would leave Egypt if the Moslems would give Jerusalem back to the Christians. The sultan said:

"Yes, if the king himself will be my prisoner until the last Crusader has left Egypt."

Louis wished to agree to this, but his nobles would not hear of it. Since there could not be peace between the armies, there was no escape for the Crusaders but by flight. Even that seemed hopeless. Still it was all that could be done. Only a few of the boats which had followed them up the Nile were left. On these they placed the sick men and all the women and children. Then by night they set them afloat down the stream towards Damietta. The nobles begged Louis to go on board one of these vessels.

"Nay, I march with the last man of mine who lives," said Louis. As the army left the camp, it was attacked. Louis turned and fought wildly for his men.

"Wait for the king! Wait for the king!" rang from the banks. The vessels were stayed, but Louis signed to them to go on. At length Louis and his men left the camp. The king was on horseback, but without helmet or cuirass. But all their efforts were in vain. Both ships and soldiers fell into the hands of the enemy. The king was weak and ill, but still free. His knights saw that he could go no further. They sought to hide him in a house in an Egyptian town, where a humble woman from France tended him gladly. But in spite of the knights who guarded the door, the Moslems burst into the house and loaded King Louis with chains. They carried him to Mansourah in a vessel gaily decked in honour of the great prisoner they had taken. As he sailed southwards up the stream, he saw his men driven along the banks in chains.

Louis in prison was as great a man as Louis in battle. He wore a coarse robe, because he would not deign to wear the gay clothing the sultan sent to him, nor would he feast with the Moslems, though they wished him to join them.

Each day he saw some of his followers led out from prison. They were asked if they would cease to be Christians and accept the faith of the prophet. They

HOW LOUIS THOUGHT DEATH A LITTLE THING

refused. No sooner had they done so than they fell dead before the eyes of their captive king. It was a terrible thing for him to sit thus day after day and watch the men who had fought by his side, and whom he loved, slain in this barbarous way.

When the sultan thought he had tried the king so long and so greatly that he would be glad to agree to any terms, he offered him freedom if he would give to him Damietta and the cities of Palestine. Louis had won Damietta in battle, but he had no right to the cities of the Holy Land.

"The cities do not belong to me but to God," he said.

Then the sultan threatened to torture Louis to make him yield.

"I am the sultan's prisoner," said the king; "he can do with me as he will."

He was so calm and firm that a Moslem who stood by said: "You treat us, sire, as if you had us in prison instead of our holding you."

But though the sultan spoke of torturing King Louis, he did not do it except by making him watch the men of his army as they died before him. When he found that the king would not yield he gave in himself, and agreed to accept Damietta in return for the king, and a large sum of money for those of the army who still lived.

But the knights would not let Louis wait to see the men set free. A vessel lay waiting at the mouth of the Nile. As soon as he and his queen were on board, it sped out to sea, and ere long King Louis was once more in France.

He was a great ruler as well as a great fighter, and he thought of the needs and duties of those whose king he was, as none in that land had ever done before. While he made France strong and its people happy, Bibars, who had so cleverly trapped Robert at Mansourah, became sultan, and laid waste the Holy Land. The news of this reached the northern lands from which the crusading armies had gone forth in former days, and once more the great longing to save Jerusalem took hold of Louis. His nobles sat in council. He came to them bearing a crown of thorns in his hands. Again he fastened the cross of war on his shoulder. He had heard that a great king in Africa was willing to become a Christian, and as he thought of this he dreamed bright dreams. He thought that he might bring this desert king and his dark followers to join his faith and his army, and that with them to aid him, he might even yet conquer the Moslem armies and win Jerusalem and Palestine.

His fleet sailed for the African coast. The army landed and marched into the desert. The hot sand blew about them and choked them. They found no friendly welcome, but only messages of blood and war from the king whom Louis had hoped would join him in battle against the Moslems. Illness and death swept through the army. One of the first to die was a son of King Louis. Soon the king himself lay dying in his tent in the hot desert camp.

"Jerusalem, Jerusalem," he cried, "we will go to Jerusalem!" His couch was very comfortless, but it was

HOW LOUIS THOUGHT DEATH A LITTLE THING

not so humble as Louis wished it to be. He bade them spread ashes on the ground and lay him there. When they had done this, they saw his lips more. They bent to listen, and heard these words:

"Father, into Thy hands I commend my spirit."

Then he fell asleep. The sleep grew deeper and deeper, and soon the men who watched him there knew that he would never wake on earth again.

In the dim light of the tent, on a bed of ashes, lay all that was left of good King Louis. His beautiful face still kept the grandeur men had loved to see all his life long. He lay there in the sad, plague-stricken camp, and around him there seemed to linger the light of heaven.

Louis was the last of the heroes of the Crusades, but for years after his death the Christian forces held cities in the Holy Land. At last they were driven from all their strongholds, and the Moslem rule was unbroken.

To-day there is no kingdom of Jerusalem. There are ruins of churches and of castles, and the broken walls show how great was once the power of the armies of the Cross.

But though the dream of the Crusaders never came true, and though all their efforts left little mark on the life of the East, yet the lands from which the knights went out have been changed, and all their history has been different, because of those wars to which their armies went.

Over the door of an old house in a close in Edinburgh a scallop-shell, like the shells that were brought by pilgrims from the Holy Land, was cut in stone. In that house those who had made the long journey to the East, and had come back weary or ill, were welcomed and cared for. The shell above the door stood for hundreds of years to tell of the olden days. It is so in the history of Europe. Those who know it best can see the mark of the Crusades cut into the life of the nations whose knights led the armies of the Holy War, as clearly as the scallop-shell was cut into the old wall in Edinburgh.

www.ingramcontent.com/pod-product-compliance
Lightning Source LLC
Chambersburg PA
CBHW020017050426
42450CB00005B/520